I0453856

POCKET
FULL OF
SOLDIERS

POCKET
FULL OF
SOLDIERS
AND OTHER WAR POEMS

MARY LOU SINKEY

Pocket Full of Soldiers: And Other War Poems
Copyright © 2023 Mary Lou Sinkey

ISBN: 979-8-218-29258-4

First Edition

Library of Congress Control Number: 2023918464

Cover & Interior Design/Layout and Publishing assistance provided by: Crystal Heidel, Heimat Publishing

All Cover Images from Unsplash.com

Front Cover Image by Eduard Delputte
Back Cover Image by Holly Mindrup

Printed in the USA on acid free paper.

ACKNOWLEDGMENTS

A special thank you to my teachers at the Rehoboth Beach Writers Guild, particularly to poet Gail Comorat, whose encouragement went above and beyond. Sincere thanks to Ellen Collins, poet extraordinaire, who edited my poems and offered wise advice. A warm thank you to Crystal Heidel of Heimat Publishing for her expertise in assisting in my publication of this chapbook.

My love and gratitude to my husband, Bill, and my children, for their generous and loving support. Their encouragement throughout this endeavor was invaluable.

DEDICATION

Dedicated to my father, Dominick Anthony Longobardi (1918-1988) who served in World War II in the United States Army, 60th Infantry, 9th Division. He was wounded in the African Campaign on the beaches of Oran during Operation Torch. My hero in war and peace.

Many and sharp the num'rous ills
Inwoven with our frame!
More pointed still we make ourselves,
Regret, remorse, and shame!
And man, whose heav'n-erected face
The smiles of love adorn, -
Man's inhumanity to man
Makes countless thousands mourn!

From "Man Was Made to Mourn: A Dirge"
-Robert Burns, 1784

TABLE OF CONTENTS

POCKET FULL OF SOLDIERS

...'tis good also to learn from those who speak aright.
from Antigone by Sophocles

(My shrink says I am trying to find my emotions. I'm not a violent person and I don't want to think too hard about what I've seen ("a man turned to pink vapor"). I took what my duty was at the moment and if I get deployed again, so be it . . . In a dream, I'm fishing in a beautiful stream and my wife comes up and taps me on my shoulder. I grab her and cut her to pieces and then calmly serve her to the fish. But, like I said, I'm not a violent person).

This is my first entry—as told to me by a young soldier—in my "Dear America" diary that I keep in my pocket. I volunteer at the USO lounge at a nearby air base. Many pass through, leaving pieces of their lives.

I have a pocket full of soldiers.

The Vietnam vet who sleeps behind trash containers, wearing flip flops, even in the brutal cold of winter *(. . . forgotten by those I served to protect; treated like shit when I came home; my brothers on the Wall).*

Handsome, oh so handsome, tall, blonde, a Navy SEAL who made me wish I was young again *(. . . I fear the unknown of my future as a citizen, no longer a warrior).*

The retired sailor who lives on a boat in California and serves as Captain to high-paying customers *(. . . I never let death get to me; the open seas bless me with open sky).*

The soldier in Army dress greens, forlorn *(. . . I am waiting to escort the family of my crew chief to bury their son at Arlington).*

The captain who awarded me a coin of his Artillery platoon (. . . *We thank you for your service, Ma'am)*; imagine that—thanking ME for my service!

Omar, a Navy SEAL who mailed me two coins, his thank you for driving him and his wife to the Philadelphia airport (he wrote . . . *you are my hero because you refuse to forget me and my brothers who fight for freedom).*

The retired Air Force author who journals his demons; (he did not talk much to me).

The Green Beret, retired to get out of warrior mode (. . . *my wife basically gave me an ultimatum).*

Keep them in your hearts, a General said to me after the deployment ceremony of the 150th Engineer Company before they left for Afghanistan.

The retired Marine, a former Honor Guard for President Reagan, now working at Arlington.

The young airman I named "Puddin'" (his last name was Hastings). He rewarded me with a smile each time I pronounced his new moniker.

The woman on disability from the backwoods of Alabama who never knew what a shoe was until she joined the Army (and what a beautiful velvet accent).

The female Marine, tiny, seemingly frail who packs parachutes and tests them (yes, jumping from the plane is part of her tests).

The retired Navy SEAL who lost too many of his young friends, thinking they would be around to share war stories as old and frail men.

I have not been there
   to witness the cold fog that obscures their vision
   to hear RPGs explode nearby
   to taste kicked up dirt, coating everything
   to trek up a treacherous mountain back to the FOB, its white rock
      like claws
   to sit on a Humvee that hugs narrow trails, deep ravines on the
      immediate right
   to return home with a brother,
   parts only in a body bag.

But I have their stories in my pocket.

And I open my diary
   to you, I tell their stories
   to introduce you to them
   to ask you to listen
   to make them live in your mind
   to combine your hopes with theirs
   to pray there is no longer a need for war.

PREFACE

My father served overseas during World War II but never spoke of war. When I questioned him about his experiences, he offered no response. His silence was loud.

Through my poetry, I hope I have honored all our veterans, past and present; and that I have spoken respectfully for my father.

Mary Lou Sinkey, Fall 2023

ONE I SERVED

Be kind, for everyone you meet
is fighting a great battle.
      -Philo of Alexandria

I don't do much at the USO.
I offer snacks, coffee, soft drinks—
and a smile, softer than any afghan
of pure Scottish wool.

I listen.
I pose no questions.
I offer no advice. But

I can see.
I can tell.

I've met many Vets who
have escaped the hallowed womb
of Arlington, but none
have avoided
the wounds of war.

Johnny R, 25, a gunner
with the 173rd Airborne
served two deployments
in the Korengal Valley.
We talk for hours while he waits
for a C-5 to return him to his base
in Aviano, Italy.

He shakes his head—tells me
he can't think too much
of the violence he has seen.
(men I fought beside pulverized by firepower).
He changes the subject.
We talk about his newborn daughter.

These many years later,
I think often of this young warrior.
I envision an eagle in the sky,
his wings, a splendid stretch of valor,
their shadows majestic silhouettes
beneath a white-clouded ceiling,
gliding in a broad arena of freedom.

No wind   no sound
a solitude few understand.
It is only his descent to his aerie,
a place of rest
where this bird of prey
faces boundaries.

LONGBEARDS

My maiden name depicts strength, its form and meaning based on
the muscle of warriors long gone. The men away at war, the women
tied woven straw beards to their faces, to appear ferocious, to protect
the village. The enemy came and asked "Who are these long beards,
these longobardi"? They retreated in fear. I think of the longobardi and
imagine the might of Samson. I include my father, a soldier engaged
in Operation Torch while Rommel's red, black and white-circled flag
whipped in the wind, shamelessly.

On the shores of Oran—
the silhouette of death
unwelcome by your side.

I learn of war from my father but not through conversation—my
curiosity sated from the pages of books. I witness despair, I cry with
those who lose their friends and those who save them. I feel the enemy's
heated and hated breath upon my neck. Despite all this, I am naive. In
truth, I know nothing of the bane of war. We have never met.

Hell visits—
birds are silenced
by the screams.

Before the war, my father captained the local baseball team; he knocked
out a professional middleweight champion; and he carried a piano on
his back from a bar his family owned. Then war came. He was shot, his
leg shattered, but he never fully healed—his vigor no longer present.
He did not seem like a longobardi to me.

Men storm the beaches—
bodies wounded, the dead
misplaced along the water's edge.

I understand my dad more—long after he is gone. Inside the pages of war books, I imagine his struggle, gear heavy on his back. I see him pound the beaches, hear the cries of men beside him.

Devils and angels collide—
they choke and fall
onto the sand.

MEMORIAL DAY, 1969

To all who served and the many who gave the ultimate sacrifice during the Vietnam War.

The hometown crowd lines each side of the boardwalk. Local bands march, their uniforms an array of colors, navy and white, blue and yellow, maroon and black. The jackets have snappy gold buttons and each band shows their high school insignia. The metal badge on their tall hats shine, the plumes sway as they march in unison. They enliven us, the snare drums lending a precision in step and sound as majorettes twirl and toss batons with unmatched speed—we gasp at almost-missed catches.

Veterans wounded during battle sit on the backs of convertibles, waving to a hometown crowd. We respond with deafening cheers. They are followed by a marching assembly of robust veterans who receive loud ovations, survivors of World Wars I and II. The Korean War veterans march by next—cheers reach the sky. A final formation of soldiers are the youngest, the Vietnam veterans. They march erectly and proud but the crowd has lost its voice.

A symbol of remembrance
A red poppy bled this day
The injustice of silence.

BITTER PANCAKES

I sit in a diner
same familiar booth
pancakes before me
covered in thick syrup
topped with sweet butter,
coffee is hot
perfectly brewed
bit of cream, no sugar.

I spot four soldiers
in clean, crisp fatigues
comfortable
self-assured in their dress.
Folks pass by me without a glance
like many years ago.
Yet, for these soldiers,
they pause.

When I returned
my thanks was spittle,
a citizen's sentiment
landing on my chest.
Others turned from me
as though I were contaminated.

A dark night, long ago
monsoon-like rains pounded the earth
my fatigued body mud-smeared
hiding in a fox-hole
with my buddy
all shot up, unrecognizable.
No ammo, radio dead, isolated
awaiting reinforcements.

Sally refills my coffee
as a forkful of pancakes
is taken in
their sweetness lost.
I push the plate away.
I get up from my table
to pay the bill.

I resent the merit given them
but suddenly I imagine
these young warriors, green
targets in a god-forsaken mountain valley
steel wasps buzzing by.

As I pass their table
they look at me
they see the stump of my arm
and notice my hat, Vietnam Veteran.
I want to growl
what the hell are you looking at
but I envision them
mangled, bloody and ugly.

Their God will not protect them
For war is war and
its teeth bite ever so deeply.
I pull a fifty from my wallet,
place it on their table.
I meet their eyes and nod.

NECKLACE FROM VIETNAM

Twenty-five veterans arrive from their rooms to the VA
community center for an annual Veterans' Valentine Dance.

We pin a carnation on each—bright red against ghostly countenances.

Most are wheelchair-bound; several lie prone, blankets covering
their injuries; others shuffle toward the live band.

Vibrations from a bass guitar along with the booming beat of drums
bounce off oak-stained floors—echoes of whup, whup, whup,
drab olive Hueys that once inserted them deep into enemy territory,
the jungle-damp of the Central Highlands.

I spot Earl, his name tag as crooked as his teeth, his earlobes long,
swinging back and forth as his head bobs to the music.

Hi Earl—his smile meets mine.

*My name is Earl but drop the "L"- just call me Ear. I earned that name.
Sliced off ears of dead gooks. Personal kills. I wove them on a string
of hemp, rubber trophies around my neck.*

I imagine his necklace of ears flapping against his chest—keeping
  stride;
ears resembling seashells, twisted pretzels, each edged with brittle
  blood.

*Yep, I talked to those fuckin' ears every night, my own assembly of hearers.
During firefights, I subjected them to screams, shrieks, and shrill cries
of their men—and the high-pitched blood arias of their wives and babies
crouched in muddy canals.*

He tilts his head, reaches to pull me closer.

Ya know, lil lady, war makes us do things we never dreamed we'd do.
But those ears sure made me feel like I done somethin' for America
and I don't regret it one bit.

Our attention turns to the band as they start singing "Thirsty Ears".
Ear winks at me, his smile a perfect U,
stretched from ear to ear.

IN-COUNTRY LETTER

Variation I

I write a letter   from America to Vietnam
I meet him in a letter   from Vietnam to America

It starts out on a whim   an adventure
A giddy silly girl of 16

It is 1969   most friends do not talk about Vietnam
I never stop

I discovered Vietnam six years prior
My fifth-grade teacher

As though that lesson brought me to this moment
I am for the war   I am against the war

The domino theory is plausible
Killing dictators at whim is not

I send Christmas greetings
I add my return address

Simple words form my letter
I tell him I pray for him

I know many at home do not
They protest   prayers lost in a fog

He tells me in-country is chaos   death
His letter is long

He asks that I write   take his mind off war
A leader   young   leading younger men

He wants to sustain their morale
The monsoon season does not help

Their feet never dry   socks   what's left of them
pull off with heels attached

I don't tell him home is chaos
Rock and roll   drugs   disrespect

Disregard for those like him
Who wear their hair short

Who wear a uniform and carry a rifle
Who serve and suffer   who die

I am for the war
I am against the war

War   a dark bloody horror   like all others
Men maneuver in muds of hell

On mountain tops
In the valleys

In the jungle
On the trail

The rain never ceases
Marching   marching   marching

Valor   freedom   loneliness   despair
Tracers   helicopters   ambushes   rifle jam

Heat   humidity   tigers   black pajamas
And the rain pounds   and pounds   and pounds

It never lets up
Filling every crevice   earth   body   wound

I write back   from America to Vietnam
I never hear from him again

Whenever it rains I think of him
Whenever it rains I think of war

IN-COUNTRY LETTER

Variation II

Whenever it rains, I think of war.

It begins at a sleepover. 1969. A group of teenagers, hair curlers piled high on our heads, the non-stop chattering—about boys.

Frannie tells us she sends Christmas cards to troops in Vietnam. This captures my attention.

Writing to a strange boy in a war that most despise seems daring. The next day, I begin my letters and include my return address. I select a box of cards, each with the same evening scene. A simple Christmas tree on the front, unadorned—a bright star atop disperses its light. With my favorite blue-ink fountain pen, I complete fifty. I slide each into an envelope, ready to mail.

Will they write back? What will I write next?

Time passes. I start to believe no letters will come until one day I receive two. I run into my bedroom, shut the door, and begin to read them.

From Saigon. *Thanks for your Christmas greetings. I am from Hawaii and happy to know those on the mainland pray for us. Aloha!*

From Okinawa. *Thanks for the Christmas card . . . I grew up near Wildwood. Send me a picture of you on the beach.*

More letters arrive, brief expressions of sincere thanks. But one is several pages long.

From Pleiku. *Thank you for your sweet letter . . . It is monsoon season and the rain is pounding outside my tent. I seek solace within these small walls, away from my men. As their leader, they look up to me. I cannot show them my hand-wringing despair, but it has become difficult.*

I put the letter down. After some minutes, I pick it up and continue to read.

We are threatened daily by the enemy, very tired and always wet. Please write to me. I know a correspondence will help make my days more bearable and bring about some normalcy in-country.

I put the letter in a drawer. I try not to remember his name but cannot stop thinking of the young Lieutenant. I tell no one about his letter and finally decide to not answer.

Some days later, I come home from school drenched. *It has been raining all day. . . . the rain is pounding . . . I am weary and so are my men.*

I go to bed early and slip into white sheets, they smell like roses. I pull the blankets up and lay my head on a soft pillow. It is especially dark tonight. The continued sound of rain. I stare into darkness; I envision my new friend, cold, wet, weary. *We have been marching all week in the rain under the weight of heavy gear. Our shoes and socks, what's left of them, never dry. Some men take them off and pull the heels of their feet with them.*

The next day, I mail a letter. Days grow into months.

I look forward to corresponding with you. Sincerely, First Lieutenant . . .

I never know what happened to the young Lieutenant. I never hear from him again.

These many years later, I often think of him. And, I recall a once naïve young girl, unexpectedly brought closer to the darkness and pain of war.

WORLDS APART

I.

A small town in New Jersey
February 2, 1968

Another Kindergarten day is over
We hustle to put on our winter wear
Racing about for a quick retreat
Like soldiers after battle

Outside I stand alone
Others run to their parents' cars
Or begin their walk home
I peer down the street
My ride yet to appear

No one is about
Even my teacher has driven away
The cold is numbing
My surroundings as quiet as a prayer room

The locked gray concrete
Building adds no color
As I huddle on its steps
My warm red coat in bold contrast

I feel a fear of abandonment
But then—
A cloud of white roars my way
My mom at the wheel.

II.

Vietnam Hue City
February 2, 1968

During an intense Tet Offensive battle
A soldier lay dying, flung to the earth
His dark red blood
Gushing, soaking the ground

On his back, with arms stretched upward
To a God invisible
His nostrils flare
A lack of oxygen
Increased effort to breathe
He wheezes   his face blue

Tears fall—he cries softly, mourning
He knows there is no homecoming

A belch of dust erupts from the earth
A medic rushes to him
Sees no retractions of his chest
And announces another young tragedy
In somber tone—
He moves on to other wounded.

A SOLDIER'S LAST LETTER

Go and catch a falling star
And know there is more
Between the light and me
Because it is time
To calm the waters and drive away
A suffering world
Where there is neither sense of life or joys
But those of memory
Murmur, a little sadly, how Love fled
Of withered leaves about your feet
Doesn't everything die at last, and too soon
And when the time comes to let it go
Try to recall the color of the sky
And all that's best of dark and bright
Before the night falls completely over us

Sources
John Donne, "Song"
Joy Harjo, "Eagle Poem"
Emily Dickinson, "I heard a Fly buzz---when I died"
Shirley Geok-Lin Lim, "Learning to Love America"
Yusef Komunyakaa, "Kindness"
David Budbill, "What Issa Heard"
John Clare, "I Am"
Hart Crane, "My Grandmother's Love Letters"
William Butler Yeats, "When You Are Old"
T.S. Eliot, "Preludes I"
Mary Oliver, "The Summer Day"
Mary Oliver, "In Blackwater Woods"
T.S. Eliot, "Ash-Wednesday"
Paul Bowles, "Scene V"
George Gordon, Lord Byron, "She Walks in Beauty"
Nicanor Parra, "Stains on the Wall"

REMEMBER THE FALLEN

The earth wails
a necessary response
ruins of battlefields
heaps of rubble
destroyed woods and villages
desolate   haunted
this hell freezes
above and beyond the surface

Powerful photo on that wall
you understand what it can do
give voice to the voiceless
the men who shed precious
blood, sweat, and tears
freedom rings because of you
our nation's warriors

There is a lesson in everything
more than just
scarred landscapes
still telling . . .

I wrote this FOUND poem extracting the words from the following three publications: (1) *New York Daily News*, Monday February 2, 2015; (2), *Air Force Times* 26 January-2 February 2015; (3) *Air Force Times* 9 February 2015; and the book *Violence of Action: The Untold Stories of the 75th Ranger Regiment in the War on Terror* by Marty Skovlund, Jr with LTC Charles Faint & Leo Jenkins, First Edition, 2014 by Blackside Concepts.

FINAL SALUTE

Show me the two so closely bound
As we, by the wet bond of blood,
By friendship blossoming from mud . . .
                    -Robert Graves

It's temporary, this tomb of mine
a silver case draped
by the red, white, and blue
wrapped tight, its furl as still as my heart.

It's quiet but for the hum
of the C-17 Globemaster.
I, its precious cargo
soon to descend upon the soil of my birth
where once I built forts and
splashed puddles in the rain.

In the Helmand Province
southern Afghanistan
I was lead
on a foot patrol when it happened—

a bomb blast—my body
flung, twisted, a mangled mess
my face, frozen and contorted
the shock of death in every crease.

Now . . . my friends sit aside me
escort me aboard this gray might
their heads resting in their hands
stares   unblinking
the black anvil of death inside them—
thinking of the blast
thinking they should be in this tomb.

MARY LOU SINKEY

The darkness that surrounds us
must not dim our long toil
brothers, know I am free
of imperfect flesh
that once formed me—
know I am at rest
salute me as I do you.

MOVEMENT NO. 43

Today, the earth stands still, its spin halted as though held in a tight
hug
within the arms of Atlas. He will not let go; not yet. I sit in the front of
the bus,

the Chaplain next to me. We are there to assist and escort the eight
strangers
behind us to receive their loved one. We follow a slow-moving police
car,

its blue and red lights pulsate. I gaze out my window and see cars pulled
to the side, pedestrians saluting while others place a hand over their
heart.

The world appears lifeless but for a row of small pine trees, a quiet wind
sways their gentle limbs back and forth, back and forth, rhythmic
pendulums,

a symphony, a movement by God, His breath exhaling comfort
upon this family of eight. We reach the flight line. They disembark,

I study them. Their grief ages them, not one is over 50. They appear
old—
fragile bodies bent into each other for support, countenances

creased with grief—their noses red and wet. I offer tissues and cool,
damp
washcloths as the huddle of mourners take their seats and face the C-17,

a gray glare against a sapphire sky. The transfer case, covered
with a tightly wrapped American flag, is carried off the plane in quick
precision

steps. No sound but the clicks of the carry team. We welcome home
their fallen soldier—back on American soil, killed less than 48-hours
   ago in Kabul.

*.....an American soldier, 26, killed by hostile fire, leaves a wife, two
small children, father, mother, brother, sister, aunt, and uncle.*

When a fallen soldier comes home and touches the land of his birth, a
   reverent calm
receives him. The fallen soldier rests. He is at peace. The living

go on with sadness beyond telling. And God bids Atlas
to gently release his hold and set the earth back in motion.

Note: When a service member dies in theatre, he is returned within 72 hours
to Dover Air Force Mortuary, his first landing on American soil. It is known
as a Dignified Transfer and the process of receiving him home by loved ones
and those who honor him is called a Movement.

I attended Movement 43 in 2016. This poem is written in memory of the sol-
dier who came home that day. He was only 26 years old and died of wounds
received from encountering hostile enemy forces. He was supporting Opera-
tion Freedom's Sentinel.

LETTERS

I find in the corner of a drawer
letters held together by a rubber band
about to crumble

the domino theory threatened
penned during rare moments of solitude
in the jungles of Vietnam
the dark of death
unwelcome by your side

we traced your words
on thin lines of blue
one by one
bringing you nearer
touching you

the final letter is on top
arriving before the early-morning knock
birds silenced
by our screams

i see you
your warm hazel eyes
tall, handsome, smiling
dodging me as i tousle your hair
thick with curls
a gentle scent of aftershave
lingering
as you prepare for a date

ink dulled by time
i read your letters
and walk with you again
in your world
a shadow in its violence

I REMEMBER HIM

At the going down of the sun and in the morning
We will remember them…
(from "For the Fallen" by Laurence Binyon)

First car, 1969 is written on the back of the polaroid I hold, taken the day before he left for Vietnam. He was 21. I sent this picture to him while he was in-country, now yellowed with age—crinkly, each corner bent. The photo shows his Dodge Charger, pumpkin orange, a spotless sun flame in our driveway.

Years later, he talked to me about the war. *I was their leader. These boys looked up to me. I was their strength, a lion to shield his cubs. But I could not save Mikey, from Oklahoma, just 19; or Davis, who never left the hills of Alabama until he joined the Army; or Skinny, who always had a cigarette dangling from his mouth. All cut down while on patrol. I watched blood burst from their wounds, limbs mangled, lost—eyes wide, fear on their faces. I hear their wailing every day. They knew. They knew death had them.*

I watched my brother's vigor become a quiet madness. Dark memories haunted him—boys lost in their youth, the killing, the roar of death, the smell of fear. One night, he lifted a cold gun from beneath his bed, put it to his temple and pulled the trigger.

WAR CUT

I see his name on the Wall
etched in black granite
unblemished in contrast to a cloudy sky
a name unknown, unwept by most who visit here

but I know him well
he is my warrior son.

He came to me
bounced in my chair
his ponytail thick and robust
Going to war Pops
Gonna kill for America
I listened, jealous of his zeal
I buzzed his head, the clippers
a bulldozer shearing his youth.

I touch his name
I think of his smile, his voice
Don't worry Dad, I'll be home soon
his sweet smell of aftershave
as I hugged him goodbye
his wave like the flag
he vowed to defend.

Grief visits daily after sundown
uninvited—it wraps around me
I crave sunrises
their rainbowed pleated rays
reflections of pride for my son
and for those who march to new wars
storms gripped in their fists
for a new violence of action.

THE DEVIL'S PUNCH

He points upstairs, the source of the sniper—I nod.
We race, taking two steps at a time; on the top step,
he turns to say something, his eyes, a frozen stare. It is then
I see the brown hole in the middle of his forehead,
directly beneath his Kevlar helmet,
a thin river of blood forming.
He slumps, the devil's punch dropping him.

A tan and green cranium of ballistic materials
designed to protect the head

from shock waves of explosions.
But, the bitch is, the helmet's not foolproof.

You can get it right between the eyes.
When Ares, the dark slaver, spits fiery rounds,

he wields his power tearing apart flesh
while the maroon tongues of his war-devils

slurp the blood of the dying, banishing their dreams.
War is a too oft-repeated word in our history books.

As for our children?

They too will make room in graveyards
to stand slabs of gray marble for their warrior dead.

They too will bury new white bones
atop the dust of ours.

THE DYING OF TIME

There is the persistence of song
in rainfall at morning and dewfall at night.

But as it is, my wish is first to offer prayer
into the destination of the wind.

Had I the heavens' embroidered cloths
like starry velvet in the night

I would go up and wash them from sweet wells
of life, at that sweet time when winds are wooing.

I shall lean on a pillar of amethyst
so the soul can leap out

past the entanglement where hopes lay strewn,
the remnants of us.

On the breathless corridors of the nights,
one would say the hidden stars were bells

of glory for the people yet to come.
With the wind sliding past through unmeasured darkness,

I can feel the tug,
the dying of time in the white light of tomorrow.

Sources

Howard Moss, "The Persistence of Song"
Robert Louis Stevenson, "I Will Make You Brooches"
Pindar, "Pythian 3: for Hieron of Syracuse"
Allen Tate, "To the Lacedemonians"
W.B. Yeats, "He Wishes for the Cloths of Heaven"
Edwin Arlington Robinson, "The Mill"
Wilfred Owens, "Strange Meeting"
Percy Bysshe Shelley, "Hymn to Intellectual Beauty"
Paul Bowles, "Spire Song"
Isaac Rosenberg, "Daughters of War"
Wilfred Owens, "Apologia pro Poemate Meo"
Theodore Harrison, "The Storm Has Come/The Field"
Paul Bowles, "Message"
A.M. Klein, "Winter Night:Mount Royal"
Dante Alighieri, "Paradiso"
Paul Bowles, "Nights"
Seamus Heaney, "Punishment"
Theodore Roethke, "The Far Field"

WAR WOUNDS

He is pale
like sails of an old weathered ship.
I regard him before me
standing erect in his dress greens,
the crease in his pants sharp,
ribbons, rows of blues, reds, golds
against his dark jacket.

I smile at him
you look very handsome.
His smile a gentle ripple
as he stares at the floor.
My crew chief was killed
his helicopter shot down
enemy fire.

He looks up.
The beauty of his blue eyes
cannot quell the quiver in his voice.
I'm escorting him to Arlington
to meet his family
to bury their son.

Silence.

The language of war is unconventional,
life rearranged, a shiver.

Ghosts of former battles charge in protest
of those who join them—

but understand this:
They too moan and grieve
for the living,
for this soldier in his dress greens
who learns of love through loss
and recognizes death in himself.

THE KILL

(cracking sounds rush past me
bullets hit dirt and rock
i take a knee, aim and BOOM
thunder leaves my gun
punches him just above the heart
pink mist splayed
fluids of a now vaporized enemy)

dear mom,

just killed a man

we're back at the FOB, body-hard
hands steady as oil drill pumps
i toss my 5-pound helmet
and 80-pound body armor
on an old green cot
clean my metal soul-mate
and prep for the next mission
my brothers and i unwind
in the silence of the aftermath

mom, i don't know
what life will be like
once i'm home
i'll mark the latitude and longitude
exact kill spot of my first
where body parts paved
the Korengal Valley

my dear sweet mother
no time to measure emotions
they are shrapnel
embedded in my flesh

just there—hot, sharp, within

mama, do you think God hates me?

A SOLDIER'S HEART

the driver of the Humvee is green
but not me   i stand erect   dead center
the baddest of the Black Hearts

mountains envelop us   we drive
along narrow paths   rocks spitting
beneath our wheels   echoing
like bullets searching flesh

browns   tans   neutrals
blend into a dry mix
a challenge to our gray fatigues
the wind-carried dust
infiltrates every crevice

the enemy spots open targets
i'll take them on
i have my SAW
come get me you bastards   come get me
just don't make me bleed

i desire to dream of daisies
with bright yellow-centered suns
to no avail
war cut out my heart
i shudder
like the quivering body of a brother
dying

i am jolted awake
as if cold blood is thrown in my face
i am here   no longer there
i am there   no longer here
a heart fragmented
its tempo uneven with the scent
of dust and pain

The *Black Hearts Brigade* is from the 101st Airborne Division's fabled 502nd Infantry Regiment.

SCREAMING EAGLES

To the brave men of Easy Company of the 506th Parachute Infantry Regiment, part of 101st Airborne Division who fought in the Battle of the Bulge (aka Ardennes Counter-offensive), December 1944—the largest and bloodiest single battle fought by the U.S. during WWII.

My white breath lingers among secrets of the forest
Old foxholes discerned in the earth
A thin layer of snow its familiar carpet
Where once artillery rounds rained iron

Old foxholes discerned in the earth
My breathing, the only sound
Where once artillery rounds rained iron
Where once men vowed *never surrender*

My breathing, the only sound
Exhaling white breaths, the color of snow
Where once men vowed *never surrender*
To defend the Allied line

Exhaling white breaths, the color of snow
Endless shivers that icy December
To defend the allied line
On the grounds of Bastogne

Endless shivers that icy December
No gloves, feet wrapped in gunnysacks
On the grounds of Bastogne
The enemy, large snowmen looming, clad in white

No gloves, feet wrapped in gunnysacks
In the horror of the forest
The enemy, large snowmen looming, clad in white
Haunting the old men of the 101st

In the horror of the forest
Continual battles, raging, 29 days
Haunting the old men of the 101st
Agonizing wounds that splintered their lives

Continual battles, raging, 29 days
Little ammunition, few medical supplies, food scarce
Agonizing wounds that splintered their lives
In the foxholes—a roof of tree limbs and dirt

Little ammunition, few medical supplies, food scarce
I too am haunted by what occurred
In the foxholes—a roof of tree limbs and dirt
On these grounds that once held the weight of blood

I too am haunted by what occurred
I stand in silence
On these grounds that once held the weight of blood
Where death and bullets no longer threaten

I stand in silence
Touching a small stone covered with moss
Where death and bullets no longer threaten
The enemy, 70 years gone, defeated

Touching a small stone covered with moss
I witness a renewed forest, healthy with growth
The enemy, 70 years gone, defeated
Strong pines tower about me, rooted, steadfast

I witness a renewed forest, healthy with growth
A thin layer of snow its familiar carpet
Strong pines tower about me, rooted, steadfast
My white breath lingers among secrets of the forest

MARY LOU SINKEY

WAR PAINT

red-stained fangs
dig deep
hard into flesh
a hungry giant
deliverer

of the broken and
maimed
across the path
bloody
crimson carpets

my dark dance
breathless exhales
euphoria
master of conquest
master of loss

clutch the marred
scatter the spoils
smell the decay
lingering
hell-rot of death

white smoky plumes
ascend
a sacrificial prayer
the dead
trophies
of indulgence

living faces
gray and gaunt
sunken
shuffle
on battlefields

i can't say i'm proud
just doing my job

i am the father of conflict
i am the son of history
i will not retreat
i am the taker
i am the deliverer of souls. watch me—
i can do this forever.

LEST WE FORGET . . .

War's a bitch. Wear a helmet, I hear a soldier say
Steel helmets replaced by Kevlar—greater protection
they declare. But nothing prevents the strike of death
in war, its non-specific push targeting men in battle
whacking them hard upon a blood-soaked earth—
the devil's mouth opens, sucking the air from them.

The devil got in the way of their MREs, for them
a quiet moment, temporary. But it goes without saying:
the vampire of death is master infiltrator of war-torn earth,
littered with his castoffs, disallowing a harbor of protection
from the smoky lightning that belches from weapons of battle.
We do not know the instant of the snatch from devil-war, a death

blow that flattens their figures like lions in death,
the fight of the fittest gone—their roars silent. We know them
as casualty statistics, a cold account of attritions of battle.
Politicians pen the rightness of war, self-righteous designs. Many say
people of the lie always fashion a phony protection
while thousands of their devil-friends roam the earth.

Those pundits who scribe in comfort think not of a scarlet earth.
They do not accompany the soldiers or become a number in death.
Their life is assured as they sink into cushy couches, a protection
for their tender backs, their home-zone of security. Fear for them
is loss of support or the burden of spilled black inkwell on white carpet
   —they say
they mourn our dead heroes while glorifying strategies of battle.

So many dead, so many snuffed in the throes of bastardly battle—
eulogies country-wide; of sons and daughters entombed in the earth.
Let us not forget what historians should lament, a strong say
of prayerful tributes to casualties of war—unknown in life and death
by many. Pray for those desecrated on unfamiliar soil boldly tread by
    them.
War does not age; it is forever reinvented, a new predicate of protection

again by so-called leaders in their expensive garb, a warm protection
against soft skin. Meanwhile, bloody foam dribbles from Leviathan—
    a new battle
planned where he celebrates new whacks of loss. But, for politicians, for
    them
and their ilk who sit quietly—glued to iPhones while soldiers pound
    the earth
engaged in new dystopias. Cold leaders sending government issue to
    their death.
The bite of the apple is the cause, and many nod in agreement to the
    preacher's say.

New wars persist—another pseudo-protection paid by them, the naive
    citizens
who have no say in strategies of battle. Many brave victims of a dark
    slayer's wrath,
their names etched on cold marble, set aright with older giants, in the
    soft grass of earth.

(First line from *House to House: A Soldier's Memoir* by David Bellavia.)

MARY LOU SINKEY

A GIANT IN MY PATH

I roam about a disordered garden with no sense of doom.
I spot beside a rose bush a large slumbering figure, in fetal-like twist.
A giant named Freedom and I, his soldier, a collective bloom.

He stretches his arms, about to awaken—of this I presume.
They cut through air and break apart a hazy mist.
I roam about a disordered garden with no sense of doom.

Freedom stands, rising tall, his breathing a stormy boom.
His roar, bold and defiant, a frenzy to those who dare resist
A giant named Freedom and I, his soldier, a collective bloom.

His presence illumines the garden and its muddle of gloom.
I feel free, ignited, as though by a lover I have been kissed.
I roam about a disordered garden with no sense of doom.

His loud trampling echoes—he stomps an exit from this garden tomb.
But first he stops and sets his eyes upon me, nodding—he knows I exist.
A giant named Freedom and I, his soldier, a collective bloom.

I watch him depart in haste, his shadow erect—and for whom?
For us—who must join the struggle to quash Tyranny and shatter her fist.
I roam about a disordered garden with no sense of doom.
A giant named Freedom and we, his soldiers, a collective bloom.

VIVA LA RÉSISTANCE

I am a resister
Caught—in cell block 11
I am beaten   shot   raped   blood-smeared
My eyes dark like the souls who torture me
I have typhus   dysentery   gangrene
Diseases that bind me   like chains   cold   hard   biting
My skin sallow   covered in sores   pus oozing
I moan   I weep   I shriek in pain
The smell of fear   a distinct scent of ammonia
I am like a child lost   wailing for her Mother

I've been home a year now

I am alive—
Because it was not my time
Because I was lucky
Because I was spared by a blind God

I am alive—
My hair now dark   thick with curls
It smells of lemons after a fresh shampoo
My eyes   blue   crystal-like
Appealing to those who meet their gaze
My skin   pink again

But don't be deceived

I am dead—
My comrades define me
Communists   Christians   Jews
Their voices mine
Murdered   massacred   mutilated

MARY LOU SINKEY

It is maddening
When I try to live
I think of them
And die again

This poem was inspired by the book *Village of Secrets: Defying the Nazis in Vichy France* by Caroline Moorehead.

TALKS OF WAR AND PEACE

Man is explicable by nothing less
than all his history.
   -Ralph Waldo Emerson

should we?
should we not?
we should.
we should not.

The American Revolution; War of 1812;
Indian Wars; Mexican War; Civil War;
Spanish-American War; World War I;
World War II; Korean War; Vietnam War;
Desert Shield/Desert Storm; Global Wars on Terror.

agreements vanish like flash paper
handshakes, limp and damp
peace temporary
war returns

we talk of peace
we know of war.

www.ingramcontent.com/pod-product-compliance
Lightning Source LLC
Chambersburg PA
CBHW030516130626
46549CB00007B/3024